FISH

BookLife

GRACE JONES

Words that appear like **this** can be found in the glossary on page 24.

©2016
Book Life
King's Lynn
Norfolk PE30 4LS

ISBN: 978-1-78637-002-0

All rights reserved
Printed in Spain

Written by:
Grace Jones

Designed by:
Ian McMullen

A catalogue record for this book
is available from the British Library.

Contents

What are Living Things?

All living things move and grow.
Living things need air, food,
water and sunlight to
stay alive.

**These
are all
living
things.**

Frog

Tiger

Human

4

Knife, fork & plate.

Books

These are all non-living things.

Non-living things do not move or grow. Non-living things do not need air, food, water or sunlight because they are not alive.

Teddy Bear

5

What is a Fish?

Fish are living things that live in water. They need air, food, water and sunlight to live. Salmon, eels and sharks are all types of fish.

Salmon

Shark

Eel

Fish usually have fins, breathe using gills and have a backbone. They are also cold-blooded animals. This means that their body temperature changes when the temperature outside is hotter or colder.

Backbone

Fact: There are over 30,000 known species of fish.

Gills

Fins

Where do they Live?

All living things live in a **habitat** or home. Fish live in streams, rivers, ponds, lakes and oceans.

Some special fish can breathe in the water and on land. Although, they can only leave the water for a short amount of time.

This Mudskipper fish can live on land for up to three days.

Fish Homes

Fish live in many different underwater habitats around the world. A common habitat for fish are fresh water rivers. There are fewer places for them to hide from **predators** in a river so they are usually well **camouflaged**.

Thousands of species of fish live in the ocean on coral reefs. The reefs provide them with shelter from predators and places to hide so they can catch their **prey** without being seen.

Fact:
The Great Barrier reef off the coast of Australia is the largest coral reef in the world.

Coral Reef

11

What do they Eat?

A Great White shark.

Fish eat other fish or plants, or a mixture of both. Fish that eat other animals, like the Great White shark, are called **carnivores**. They use their super sense of smell to hunt out their prev from over three miles away.

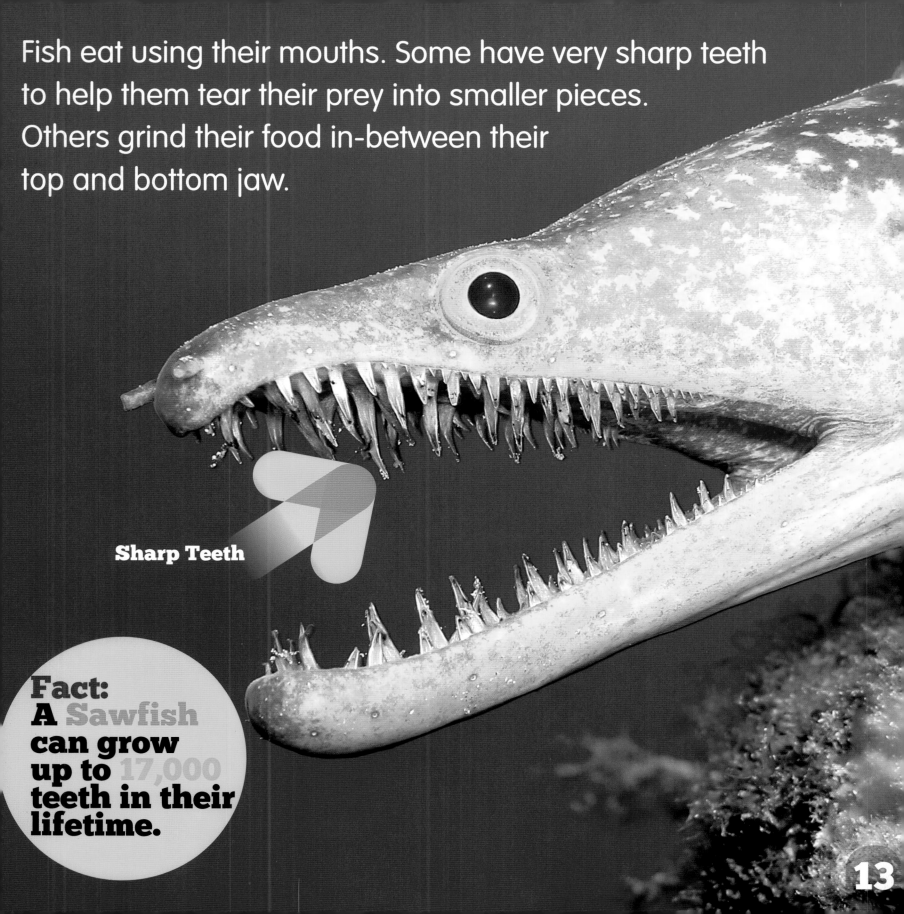

Fish eat using their mouths. Some have very sharp teeth to help them tear their prey into smaller pieces. Others grind their food in-between their top and bottom jaw.

Sharp Teeth

Fact: A Sawfish can grow up to 17,000 teeth in their lifetime.

How do they Breathe?

All fish breathe through their gills which are usually on either side of their head. They swallow water through their gills and oxygen in the water moves throughout the rest of their body.

Gills

Some fish, like the Mudskipper fish, can breathe on land too. They often breathe through their skin just like frogs and toads do.

15

How do they Move?

Fish have fins to help them swim through the water. Their tail fin pushes them through the water, whilst their other fins help them to balance, stop and change direction.

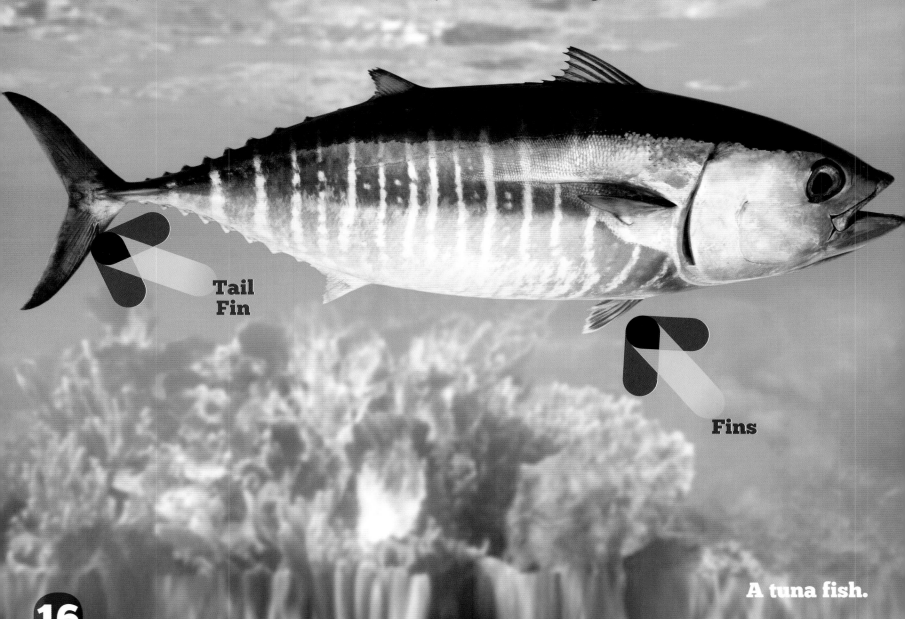

Tail Fin

Fins

A tuna fish.

Some fish, like manta rays, have their fins at the side of their bodies. They use their strong body muscles to flap their fins. When they move, they look like they are flying in the water.

Manta Ray

How do they Grow?

Most fish start life as eggs. Sometimes fish fathers look after their eggs or carry them until they **hatch**.

Male seahorses carry their eggs around with them in a special pouch.

After they hatch, their parents do not look after them. They look for shelter and food to eat on their own.

Fantastic Fish

Puffer fish protect themselves from predators by puffing up their bodies into a ball. Sharp spikes appear all over their bodies so predators do not try to eat them.

Hammerhead sharks have strange flat, hammer shaped heads. Their eyes are on each side of their head so they can see their prey wherever they are.

Eyes

World Record Breakers

WHALE SHARK

Fact: The Whale shark is longer than two buses put together!

Record: The World's Biggest Fish

Size: Up to 19 metres long

SAILFISH

Speed: Up to 68 miles per hour

Record: The World's Fastest Fish

Fact: The Sailfish swims much faster than a lion can run.

23

Glossary

Camouflaged: when an animal is hard to see because they are the same colour as their habitat.

Carnivores: animals that eat other animals rather than plants.

Habitat: a home where animals and plants live.

Hatch: when a baby animal or insect comes out of its egg.

Predators: any animal that eats other animals and insects.

Prey: any animal or insect that is eaten by another.

Index

Photo Credits